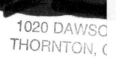

1020 DAWSO
THORNTON, C

MW00489293

I Know Fractions
by Their Actions!

Tracy Kompelien

Consulting Editors, Diane Craig, M.A./Reading Specialist
and Susan Kosel, M.A. Education

ABDO
Publishing Company

McELWAIN ELEMENTARY SCHOOL
1020 DAWSON DRIVE
THORNTON, CO 80229

Published by ABDO Publishing Company, 4940 Viking Drive, Edina, Minnesota 55435.

Printed in the United States.

Credits
Edited by: Pam Price
Curriculum Coordinator: Nancy Tuminelly
Cover and Interior Design and Production: Mighty Media
Photo Credits: ShutterStock, Wewerka Photography

Library of Congress Cataloging-in-Publication Data

Kompelien, Tracy, 1975-
    I know fractions by their actions! / Tracy Kompelien
       p. cm. -- (Math made fun)
    ISBN 10 1-59928-529-0 (hardcover)
    ISBN 10 1-59928-530-4 (paperback)

    ISBN 13 978-1-59928-529-0 (hardcover)
    ISBN 13 978-1-59928-530-6 (paperback)
    1. Fractions--Juvenile literature. I. Title. II. Series.

QA117.K66 2007
513.2'6--dc22

                                                          2006012561

SandCastle Level: Transitional

SandCastle™ books are created by a professional team of educators, reading specialists, and content developers around five essential components—phonemic awareness, phonics, vocabulary, text comprehension, and fluency—to assist young readers as they develop reading skills and strategies and increase their general knowledge. All books are written, reviewed, and leveled for guided reading, early reading intervention, and Accelerated Reader® programs for use in shared, guided, and independent reading and writing activities to support a balanced approach to literacy instruction. The SandCastle™ series has four levels that correspond to early literacy development. The levels help teachers and parents select appropriate books for young readers.

| **Emerging Readers** | **Beginning Readers** | **Transitional Readers** | **Fluent Readers** |
| (no flags) | (1 flag) | (2 flags) | (3 flags) |

These levels are meant only as a guide. All levels are subject to change.

A fraction

names part of a whole.

Words used to talk
about fractions:
equal
half
quarter
third
whole

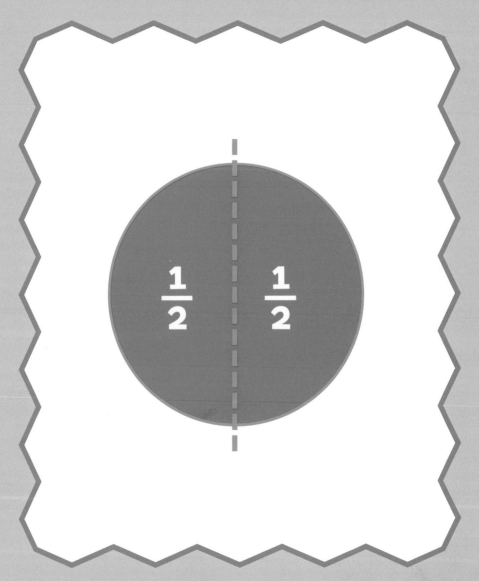

This circle has two equal parts. Each part is one half.

I know that two equal parts is the same as two halves, or the fraction $\frac{2}{2}$.

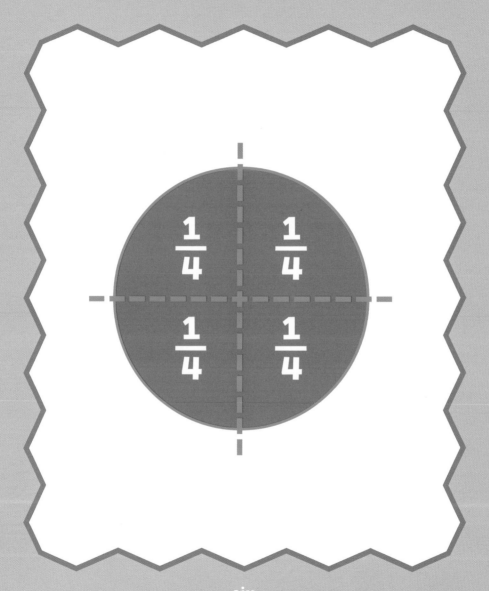

This circle has four equal parts.

I know that four equal parts is the same as four quarters, or the fraction $\frac{4}{4}$.

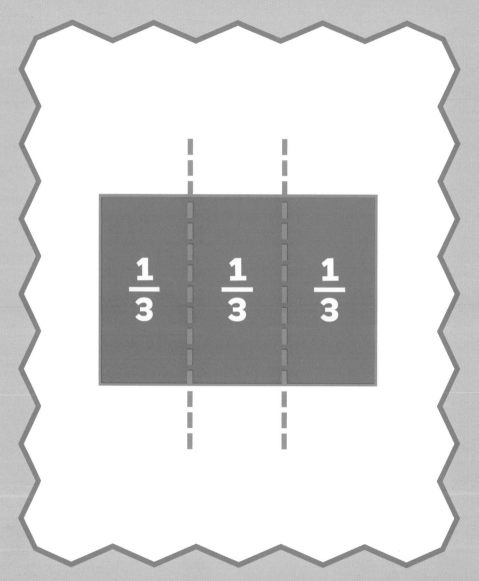

This rectangle has three equal parts, which are called thirds.

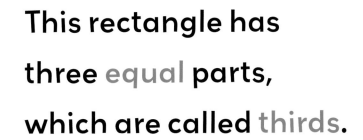

I know that three equal parts is the same as thirds, or the fraction $\frac{3}{3}$.

I Know Fractions by Their Actions!

Frank has a pizza, and it is whole.

Whole means the entire object, 1, or $\frac{1}{1}$.

twelve
12

Frank has a laugh as he cuts the pizza in half.

Half means the object is split into 2, or is $\frac{2}{2}$. If I ate half of this pizza, I would be eating $\frac{1}{2}$ of the pizza.

Two more friends want some of the order. Frank cuts it in four, and they each have a quarter.

I know that I should cut the pizza into 4 sections for 4 people. One of the sections would be $\frac{1}{4}$.

Using Fractions Every Day!

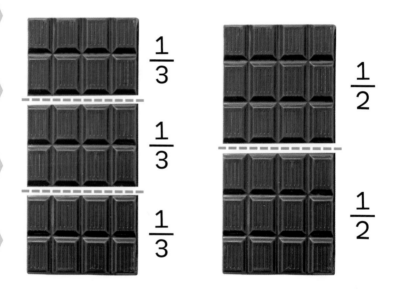

$\frac{1}{3}$

$\frac{1}{3}$

$\frac{1}{3}$

$\frac{1}{2}$

$\frac{1}{2}$

$\frac{1}{3}$ of a  is not as much as $\frac{1}{2}$ of a is.

If I split a chocolate bar with one friend, I would have more candy than if I were to split it with two friends.

There is 1 .

Francy split the apple

in . She will eat

$\frac{1}{2}$ of the apple.

I know this because there is one apple split into two parts. This means there are two halves.

twenty
20

Francy split the  into 4 parts. She will eat $\frac{1}{4}$ of the  after dinner.

The pie is split into four parts. I will have $\frac{1}{4}$ of the pie, which I also call a quarter or a fourth.

Think about what foods you like to share with your friends. What fractions do you use?

Glossary

equal – having exactly the same size or amount.

half – one of two equal parts. Half can be written as the fraction $\frac{1}{2}$.

quarter – one of four equal parts. Quarter can be written as the fraction $\frac{1}{4}$.

split – to separate or cut apart.

third – one of three equal parts. Third can be written as the fraction $\frac{1}{3}$.